Getting Him to Propose

*How to Make Your
Boyfriend Want
to Commit to You
for Life*

by Chase Scott

Table of Contents

Introduction...1

Chapter 1: Check If He's Ready........................5

Chapter 2: Make Sure It is the Right Time................11

Chapter 3: Know What *Not* to Do 15

Chapter 4: Show Him That You're Ready..................19

Chapter 5: The Fear of Marriage..................................25

Chapter 6: How to Share Your Opinions, Without Putting Pressure on Him..29

Conclusion 33

Introduction

There are a lot of women all over the world that have been in a very long relationship, but their boyfriend does not show any signs that he wants to move to the next level. Most of these women are not sure about their future and they are wondering if there is something they can do in order to make their partner propose. If you are one of these women, you should continue reading.

This book is written to help you understand how most men think, and what women can do (and women should not do) to get their boyfriend to propose.

Even if you read and follow everything in this book, of course I can't guarantee that your boyfriend will propose the very next day. However, you will at least have a better understanding of how most men think, and all the things they need to feel in order to propose. And by using this information, you will be able to influence the way your boyfriend thinks about marriage, which will make him much more likely to pop the question.

© Copyright 2014 by LCPublifish LLC - All rights reserved.

This document is geared towards providing exact and reliable information in regards to the topic and issue covered. The publication is sold with the idea that the publisher is not required to render accounting, officially permitted, or otherwise, qualified services. If advice is necessary, legal or professional, a practiced individual in the profession should be ordered.

- From a Declaration of Principles which was accepted and approved equally by a Committee of the American Bar Association and a Committee of Publishers and Associations.

In no way is it legal to reproduce, duplicate, or transmit any part of this document in either electronic means or in printed format. Recording of this publication is strictly prohibited and any storage of this document is not allowed unless with written permission from the publisher. All rights reserved.

The information provided herein is stated to be truthful and consistent, in that any liability, in terms of inattention or otherwise, by any usage or abuse of any policies, processes, or directions contained within is the solitary and utter responsibility of the recipient reader. Under no circumstances will any legal responsibility or blame be held against the publisher for any reparation, damages, or monetary loss due to the information herein, either directly or indirectly.

Respective authors own all copyrights not held by the publisher.
The information herein is offered for informational purposes solely, and is universal as so. The presentation of the information is without contract or any type of guarantee assurance.

The trademarks that are used are without any consent, and the publication of the trademark is without permission or backing by the trademark owner. All trademarks and brands within this book are for clarifying purposes only and are the owned by the owners themselves, not affiliated with this document.

Chapter 1: Check If He's Ready

What does it take for a man to propose?

According to most relationship experts, it takes <u>two things</u> for a man to propose:

1. First of all, of course, it's the right woman. Now, don't panic. Since you have been going out for a long time, it's highly likely that he's already found the right woman.

2. Now the second factor, which is equally important: His "readiness" to commit. Keep in mind this is not related to you in any way, or your long-term relationship with your beau. It also has very little to do with the actual length of time you have been dating. It doesn't matter if it's been six months, a year, two years, or even five years. He's either ready to move to the next step, or not.

So what does it take for a man to be "ready"?

All men are not created equal. So stop comparing yourself to your friends, and your boyfriend to your friend's husband. Your boyfriend is unique just like everyone else, so treat him that way. It takes different things for different men to become ready. However, most men want to become financially stable before they propose. They want to be prepared not only to have a wife, but also to have a family with kids that he can support.

On the other hand, some men simply want to have a bit more fun before settling down. Everybody knows that once you get married and have a family with kids, you won't be able to be quite as free to have fun on your own terms, as much as before. This often times is related to the man's age, and often times it's related to the relationship status of his male friends. If your boyfriend is somewhere between 22 and 30 years old, he might just not want to start a family yet. Again, you should not forget that this has nothing to do with you.

How to check whether or not he's ready?

There are some signs that can hint that your boyfriend may be nearing readiness to propose:

- He has a good job and he is financially independent. If he is not happy with his current salary or he has financial troubles, it might be the reason why he hasn't proposed to you yet. Again you should know that your boyfriend wants to be prepared not only to live with you, but also with the children you may have together.

- He has his own house where he can start a family, or a stable and nice living situation.

- He is willing to do anything for you. He is willing to move somewhere together with you, travel anywhere with you, change his plans for you, pick up things from the store for you, etc.

- He is tired of partying and frequenting bars. Some studies show that the mature man who's ready for marriage actually prefers to spend evenings with his partner in a quiet environment rather than in loud bars with a bunch of drunk folks around.

- He has at some point expressed the desire to become a parent. Most men have a desire to become a father sooner or later. You can see if he's ready or not by the way he talks about children.

- He acts like your husband, not your boyfriend. There comes a time in the relationship where your boyfriend starts to act like he is your husband, especially in the way he becomes more comfortable around you and he starts to let you see his everyday flaws. This is another sign that he is ready and that he has already found the right woman in his life.

As mentioned at the beginning of this chapter, being ready is very important for your boyfriend in his preparation of proposing. Thanks to these signs, you may be able to tell whether or not he's "ready."

If you don't see some of these signs, there are still few things you can do to show him that you want him to propose that may help him get there faster. You can tell him that you don't expect him to financially support the entire family alone once you get married, and that he can always count on you to contribute. You can also mention that his financial position will never influence your love towards him. There are lots of different ways to express these points, either directly or indirectly. Find your own way of calming down his fears and making him feel comfortable enough to propose. Remember, showing your support means a lot to your boyfriend.

Chapter 2: Make Sure It is the Right Time

Now once you're fairly confident that he's "ready" as described in the previous chapter, you need to make sure the timing is good. *What does this mean?* Many boyfriends want to propose but they delay proposing because there is something else either important or distracting happening in their life at that particular time. *But what can be more important than proposing and starting a family?* Nothing is more important than that, but some conflicts at work, such as a big project that's weighing on him or stressing him out may keep your boyfriend focused on it and very busy. Remember, women usually determine their success in life as a factor of the relationships they have built and are able to sustain; whereas men usually determine their success in terms of their job, career, or professional progress and position. It's just different for men, and you need to show respect and understanding in order to portray that you would be supportive down the road in your marriage.

Is it the right time?

How do I know if it is the right time? Unfortunately you do not know everything that's happening in your boyfriend's life. Yes, you have been together for a long time, but that does not mean that he shares *everything* with you. There is always part of his life that you don't know about. It might be part of his job, part of his future plan, part of his hobbies or something else. However, there are some signs that can show you it may be the right time for him to propose. After you make sure he's ready to settle down, here is another list that shows it's the right time:

- He is discussing the future with you. This is the major sign that he wants to propose to you. If he's discussing long-term plans that means he sees you in his future and he wants to spend the rest of his life with you. This is the number one sign. If he's discussing the future together with you, then you have nothing to worry about.

- He is spending a lot of time with you. This means that everything else in his life is fine and he can afford to spend a lot of time with you.

- He is generally happy with his job. He comes home happy and does not complain a lot about it. If he is not happy then he might be looking for another, better job. As you know in the first chapter, he needs to have a stable job and be financially independent in order to be ready to propose.

- He drops hints about proposing to you. This means he's both ready and it is the right time *but* he may not be quite sure if *you* are ready. *How can I show him that I'm ready?* That's what Chapter 4 is all about.

* This is rare, but if he actually initiates conversations about marriage or your wedding, then this is a big "I am going to propose soon" sign. In this case, you really need to respond the right way and show him that you are ready.

If you see all or most of these signs, then again, you really have nothing to worry about. He will likely propose sometime soon.

Chapter 3: Know What *Not* to Do

Pay close attention to the following list. This "NEVER TO DO" list is very important, and if you do any of these things you are in jeopardy of actually ending your relationship instead of getting him to propose.

Absolutely avoid doing these things if you want your boyfriend to propose:

- Do not give him an ultimatum. This is not something a lot of women do, however it is the biggest mistake that you could ever make. If you do give him an ultimatum, 9 times out of 10, your relationship will end. If you are sure that he's in love with you, but you are not quite sure if he's ready to propose, then it is better to wait than to give him an ultimatum.

- Do not point out unhappily-married couples and say things like "I hope we don't end up like them." This will only bring to his attention all the risks associated with marriage.

- Do not make him jealous. Some women think that by hanging out with other men, they will make their boyfriend jealous which will force him to propose. This is another very big mistake that you can make. By doing this, it is much more likely that he'll instead break up with you, rather than propose.

- Do not compare your relationship to another one. Don't say things like "We have been going out longer than this married couple." He will understand what you are saying, but again, it will put a lot of pressure on him. You do not want to force your boyfriend to propose. You want him to do it because he *wants* to commit to you and settle down with you.

- Do not ask your friends or his family to talk with your boyfriend and find out what he is up to. You should know that this would also put pressure on him. Your boyfriend will understand that it is your question coming out of your friend's mouth since it's a direct question that has never been asked before. And even if he doesn't catch on, he won't like the pressure and it will cause him to think twice about proposing altogether.

- Do not ask him to propose to you. This will show that you are desperate to be married, and that is not an attractive quality. Never show that you are desperate. The fact that he has been with you for a long time shows you that he's in love with you. As stated in the beginning, it takes the right woman and readiness for a man to propose. Whenever you feel desperate, think about this and calm down. Be patient, not desperate.

Chapter 4: Show Him That You're Ready

First of all you need to know that pretty much every man wants to spend the rest of his life with the special someone he loves. But you should not force him to propose and settle down. That's why the first two chapters are very important before you start showing him that you're ready and you want him to propose. You have to make sure he is ready and it is the right time before you start dropping big hints about your future. If you talk frequently about having family and settling down, you might discourage him and put a lot of unwanted pressure on him. But again, all men are NOT the same and this does not apply for all of them. The one thing that all men are afraid of is rejection. Without showing him that you want to be his wife, some men will never propose. This is why this chapter is one of the most important ones.

If your boyfriend is not ready then you should not force him at all. Be patient, give him some time, but always stand by him and show your support for him.

If your boyfriend does seem ready, and it is the right time, then it is your turn to show him that you are ready.

How can you show him that you are ready?

The biggest mistake the women make is when they play mind games, and somehow think that men will understand. Don't do that. Most men prefer it when you say the same thing you mean. If your boyfriend is someone with whom you can speak about anything and everything (and he should be since this is the guy you want to be married to for life!), then you might want to have a conversation about your future together. You can ask him about his future plans. This way you show him that you are looking forward to the future and you want to be a part of his. Having a calm and mature conversation is the best sign you can give him that you want to move the relationship to the next level. If he wants some time to think about it and figure things out, then let him have that time. Again, do not put any pressure on him.

Another thing you can do is discuss the idea of eventually having children. As everybody knows, with marriage often comes starting a family. You can talk with your boyfriend and ask him to share his opinion about being a father down the road.

In general, try to act like you are already his wife, by being supportive about the things that are important to him. Don't just pretend that you care about what he does. Instead try to understand why that is important to him. Once you are his wife, you will have to support him all the time, so understanding what he is passionate about and showing him how much you care are paramount qualities to have and demonstrate regularly. Prove to him that you are mature enough to be his wife and the mother of his children.

Talk about your future and mention him. Show him that you see him as an important part of your future. You might have been going out for a very long time, but if it is the first time you're talking about your future together, then he might not be prepared and might act a bit strange. There's nothing to worry about, it's completely normal. That might be the *Fear of marriage* coming to the surface. You will understand more about this in the next chapter.

What can I do apart from understanding and supporting him?

There are a few other things you can do to send him the signals that you want him to propose. Of course, the biggest "PROPOSE TO ME" sign you can give him, is to talk about moving in together if you don't live together already. Now this is a sign he cannot miss.

However if you live together already, then you can surprise him with a few days on a little romantic road trip, or mini-vacation, or anything else that will show how much you care and that you want to spend the right of your life with him. This trip should not include any of your friends or family, it's just for the two of you.

Chapter 5: The Fear of Marriage

As mentioned in the previous chapter, some men are afraid of proposing because they are afraid of rejection. Of course you can help him to get rid of this fear if you use some hints and show him that you want him to be your life partner.

But, there is one more fear that most men have. It's the fear that being married will change your relationship, and change his life (for the worse). This is expected because marriage brings a lot of changes. It brings a new family, more responsibilities, and it's perceived to bring less fun, especially once the kids are here. As mentioned in Chapter 1, being ready is often related to the age of your boyfriend and so is the fear of marriage. If your boyfriend is somewhere between 22 and 30 years old, he might not want to start a family yet. He still wants to have fun and hangout with his friends. However once a man gets older, the fear of marriage usually naturally disappears. Instead, they look forward to getting married and settling down. But again, not all men are the same, so there is no magic number when he is sure to have overcome the fear. Again, you should not forget that this has nothing to do with you.

What can you do to help him overcome the fear of marriage?

There are few ways you can help him overcome this fear and you can do that by proving to your boyfriend that marriage is not bad at all, and married people are still happy and fun-loving people. Here is a short list of some things you can do:

- Invite a happily-married couple over for a lunch or a quiet dinner. Once he sees that there is still happiness and laughter after their wedding, he might change the way he thinks about it. And of course, you should try to avoid unhappily-married couples as much as you can.

- Watch a movie that features a happily-married couple.

- You can make logical arguments about all the benefits of marriage if he is a logical thinker. This way you also show him that you are smart and thoughtful.

- Point out older happy couples when you're together. Of course not every day, but just once in a while. Mention that you hope to be as happy as they are when you are their age.

- Show him that you want to spend the rest of your life with him. The previous chapter explains everything you need to know. The divorce rates are pretty high, so men tend to think not just twice, but many more times before they propose. Show him that you are "wife material" and you are good enough to be the mother of his children.

These are only some of the ways you can show him that marriage is a positive change, and make him look forward to it instead of being afraid.

I should also mention that there are men that just don't really believe in marriage. They don't think it is a good idea, and therefore it's going to be much harder to make that kind of guy propose to you. However, it is not impossible. As stated in the beginning, there is not much you can do to make your boyfriend "ready" to propose. But what you can do is to help him see the fundamental reason behind marriage, all the benefits from getting married, and help him to overcome his fears. These are some of the things that might influence the way he is thinking about marriage and hopefully make him understand that it is not only about him, but about you too.

Chapter 6: How to Share Your Opinions, Without Putting Pressure on Him

As mentioned in Chapter 3, you should not ask your boyfriend to propose. That way you show that you are desperate and this also puts a lot of pressure on him.

How you can tell him you want him to propose, without putting pressure on him?

Now there are few ways he can hear your opinion about marriage without you putting pressure on him at the same time. In fact, by saying your opinion, you might actually help him to overcome the fear of marriage and propose you much faster. Here are few situations that are likely to happen, and you should be prepared for them:

- When you two are part of a group of people, someone might start a topic about weddings or marriage. This is the opportunity you have to state your opinion without putting any pressure on your boyfriend.

- When you are at a wedding it is possible that someone will start a conversation about it.

So basically, whenever *SOMEONE ELSE* stars a conversation about it and your boyfriend is around. This way you get a chance to state your opinion, yet he's not the one you're talking to directly. Therefore you aren't putting any pressure on him, nor do you show that you are desperate.

What should you say exactly?

Your opinion matters a lot to him. It is true that men aren't the best listeners, but when it comes to this, sometimes they actually pretend not to listen. So rest assured, what you say on this topic, he will hear for sure. *Keep in mind all men are not the same.* Some men want big weddings, some want small ones. Since you don't know what your boyfriend wants yet, you can talk about general stuff that will make him feel much better about the wedding. What you should mention during these opportunities is that the number of people at the wedding is not very important. You can say that it is more important to have small wedding with someone that you love than have a big wedding with someone you don't. If your boyfriend is not financially stable or doesn't have the job of his dreams, you can also mention that an expensive ring is waste of money. These are just a few examples that you can use to show your boyfriend the way you're think about these topics, and also show him that he has already found the right woman.

Two things you should have in mind:

- Be sure that what you say during these conversations is what your boyfriend wants to hear about these topics. You want to show him the way you think by talking with other people, but cater your words to things that will attract him to you more, rather than scaring him off. You should know that your opinion means a lot to your boyfriend so choose your words carefully.

- Do not be the one to start these conversations. Again, by starting a conversation about weddings or marriage in front of your boyfriend, this will put him in quite an awkward position.

Conclusion

Overall, men are not as simple as women think. They have more feelings and fears than you might recognize. Men often over-think things, and most of them want everything in their life to be perfect. Since there are many things happening in their lives, you, as the girl in his life, should make an effort to prepare him to propose.

Make sure your boyfriend is ready to settle down, make sure it's the right time in his life. Show him that you want to be his wife, help him overcome his fear of marriage, and state your opinion about marriage in a way that doesn't put any pressure on him. Meanwhile, be careful to avoid saying things that will discourage him to propose.

Thanks for purchasing this book, and I hope that you choose to follow my advice. You'll have a ring on your finger before you know it! If you found the book to be helpful, I'd certainly appreciate if you'd take a moment to post a review on Amazon. Thanks again, and good luck!

Printed in Great
Britain
by Amazon